Seeing Beyond

**THE MIRACLE OF CLARITY
AND CONNECTION
IN EVERYDAY LIVING**

ADRIEN FIORUCCI

What's Real Publishing House
Wayland, NY

Copyright © 2019 by Adrien Fiorucci.

All rights reserved. No part of this publication may be reproduced, distributed or transmitted in any form or by any means, including photocopying, recording, or other electronic or mechanical methods, without the prior written permission of the publisher, except in the case of brief quotations embodied in critical reviews and certain other noncommercial uses permitted by copyright law. For permission requests, write to the publisher, addressed "Attention: Permissions Coordinator," at the following email: whatsrealpublishing@gmail.com

Adrien Fiorucci/What's Real Publishing House

Wayland, NY/14572

www.whatsrealwaf.com

Cover design by Chris Armfield of the Field, fieldart.org

Book Editing by Nathan Hassall and Deb Kastner

Book Layout ©2017 BookDesignTemplates.com

Ordering Information:

Quantity sales. Special discounts are available on quantity purchases by corporations, associations, and others. For details, contact the us at whatsrealpublishing@gmail.com

Seeing Beyond/ Adrien Fiorucci. —1st ed.

ISBN-13: 978-1-7341367-0-8

To download the FREE book

WHAT'S REAL IN RELATIONSHIPS

BY ADRIEN FIORUCCI

Visit

www.whatsrealwaf.com

Contents

About the Authentic Personal Power Series......ix

Introduction xv

Limited Perspective 1 1

   Our Six Senses 1

      The Journey of the Mind................................2

      The Dogma of our Six Senses.........................4

Limited Perspective 2 9

   Separation 9

   Avoidance 10

Limited Perspective 3 13

   Fear 13

   The Danger of the Sixth Sense 14

Before We Expand 19

Expanding Perspective 1 21

   The Dominant Sense 21

   The Conundrum 22

   Understanding Your Five Senses..................24

- Our Greatest Addiction 26
- Thought is not Reality 28
- Happiness is Not Joy 31

Contemplation for Expanding Perspective 1 35
Exercises for Expanding Perspective 1 39
Expanding Perspective 2 43
- Separation (The Way Out is In) 43
- Vulnerability and Authentic Personal Power 44
- The Barbed Wire Fence 46
- The White Picket Fence 47
- The Invisible Fence 49
- The Willingness to be Vulnerable 50
- Seeing through an Illusion 52
- The Revelation of Vulnerability 54
- The Inspiration of Vulnerability 56
- Entering a New Dimension 58

Contemplation for Expanding Perspective 2 61
Exercises for Expanding Perspective 2 64
Expanding Perspective 3 70
- Fear 70

 Knowing We Don't Know 71

 Authentic Personal Power 74

 Suffering and Inauthenticity 75

 The Two-Sided Truth 78

 Authentic 80

 Personal 83

 Power 85

 Insight and Consent 91

Contemplation for Expanding Perspective 3 93

Exercises for Expanding Perspective 3 97

Epilogue 102

Dedication:

*To every heart this finds a home.
So much depends upon you ...*

Much of what you consider to be change is nothing more than gaining a certain level of clarity and then allowing that insight to stimulate a natural response.
—Seeing Beyond, Adrien Fiorucci

"If the doors of perception were cleansed everything would appear to man as it is: infinite. For man has closed himself up, till he sees all things thro' the narrow chinks of his cavern." - William Blake

About the Authentic Personal Power Series

The *Authentic Personal Power* book series is an in-depth investigation into seven fundamental human perspectives and how they have shaped our lives and affected our everyday experience of the world. It starts by looking at the commonly held perspectives that most of us are accustomed to but may not have actually been consciously aware of. It then explores what these same perspectives might look like from an expanded point of view. Which is to say, it includes what was important and true about the original perspective and then moves on from its limits into a more inclusive and accurate assessment of each particular perspective.

As this series moves from one perspective to the next, you'll realize just how interconnected they are, and how—if one perspective is limited—they all become limited. This exploration takes place over the course of three books, allowing you, the reader, time to thoroughly digest each perspective before moving forward to the next. As with all development, the process is sequential, and is therefore beneficial to understand Perspective One before you move onto Perspective Two, then Three, etc. However, great effort has been made to ensure each perspective and book is self-contained enough to stand alone. There are times this is not quite possible, but I do believe there is still value in reading any of these works at any place and time, so you should approach them as you feel inspired.

It might be helpful to take a moment here to clarify why I have chosen to use a *six senses* model in Perspective One rather than a common five senses one. This is taken from Eastern philosophical thought, particularly Buddhism, which identifies six senses instead of five. They are as follows: eyes and visible objects, ears and sound, nose and odor, tongue and taste, body and touch and mind and mental objects. There is much that could be unpacked here, but I want to keep this simple and to the point of why I choose this model over the western one. I believe to leave out the sixth sense of the mind as part of our sensing world is a colossal omission on the part of western civilization. As I will point out later in the book, the mind is not only an important aspect of perception, it is the dominant one! This fact made it impossible for me to choose anything else. I also believe that by including the mind in our list of senses, we may already have begun to expand this perspective.

The structure of these books has been crafted to stimulate various aspects of what it means to be human. It does this by possessing three separate yet complimentary sections of each Expanding Perspective. The three sections coincide with three major movements as humans.

The first section is directed at the mind or intellect, which is to say it attempts to make sense of the perspective by means of metaphor, reasoning and clarity. The second section is aimed at the heart or emotion, which is to say, it attempts to inspire by using imagery, poetic sensibility and mystery. The third is focused on the body, which is to say it is concerned with *doing* something, even if that *doing* is simply sitting quietly and still in meditation. The point is to take what we discover and move it into the physical world through a practice or exercise.

It cannot be overstated that the third section is a critical component of this book, because far too often you simply read something and that is it. Even if you deeply enjoyed the book, it will likely have little-to-no impact on your daily life if you don't do something with it. This is why I've made sure to give three practices at the end of each Expanding Perspective. It is less important whether you actually utilize the practices suggested than it is that you should truly make forward movement by doing *something*, even if that something is of someone else's design—or better yet, your own!

Please do not let the intention of this book be squandered by relegating it to another interesting concept which gets stored away in your brain and forgotten. This life, *your* life, is far too intricate and precious to limit its wide-ranging experiences to the confines of only your mind. There is so much more to *You*, but this door remains locked unless you engage in the mystery of *You*.

Waking up the dormant dimensions of what it means to be human—or *cleansing the doors of perception*—is challenging, yet quite simple; do something different! Take on a new challenge and do so without any expectation of what is to be gained, but instead carry close to your heart the intention of reaching out beyond your current perspective to see what may lie beyond the horizon.

Be attentive. Be curious. Be You!

But be the full *You*, not just the little you. Do this and be assured you will enter new corridors, have exciting encounters and uncover elements of Yourself and the world around You that you never fathomed possible. You are immersed in a grand mystery beyond what your conventional senses can behold, and this mystery is revealed only when you expand your perspective enough to see beyond your limited concept of who and what you think you are. Only when you learn to *See Beyond* what can be seen will you ignite a fire that'll shed light into dimensions beyond your common imagining. This awakening is the stirring of your *Authentic Personal Power*, a part of you that is closer than your own breath, deeper than the DNA that determined your eye color and more powerful than you could ever imagine. *Authentic Personal Power* is the very core of who you are, and it holds the secret to a profound understanding of yourself and the world around you.

Introduction

What if all you thought was important turned out to be trivial and mundane? What if you discovered what you spend most of your time doing—what consumes most of your energy and focus—is only an infinitesimal speck of what is truly going on and pales in significance to what you could be experiencing? Furthermore, what if you found out this is already and always occurring?

Would you be interested? Would you commit to the time and energy required to discover what is really going on?

The truth is, most of us would not. Most of us already know there is something amiss in the way life is packaged, pursued and indulged in but we see no one else doing anything about it, so we feel powerless and confused in regard to how we might choose a different path. This book has been written with the sincerest intention of inspiring you. You, the person who may actually be interested in uncovering what it truly means to be a human being. The *Authentic Personal Power* series is designed to help you attain clarity and offer practical, tangible and actionable ways in which you may begin to explore the reality that has constantly been with you, but which may have eluded you up until now.

You already know *money can't buy you love, material things won't bring you happiness*, your *time here on earth is short* and you should *do unto others as you would have them do unto you.*

But if you were to take a good, honest look at yourself, what would you find? Do you truly live by these maxims? Do you spend the majority of your time on what is really important? Are you even familiar with what really *is* important? And most poignantly, are you actively, consciously living by the deepest truth inhabiting the innermost, peerless space in your heart?

For most of us the answer again is *no*. Okay, to be fair, the answer would probably sound more like, *Sort of, A little, I don't know how,* or *It just isn't practical in this day and age.*

This book is here to expand your perspective so your answer may sound more like, *Absolutely, I'm learning how more every day* or *It is amazing to me that I didn't see it before but every moment is an opportunity to discover more of who I am and what life is really all about.*

The reason why you know the truth but don't live by what you know is simpler than you may think. The *doors of perception*, as Blake refers to them, is your perspective. You are locked into a certain perspective on life, and from this vantage point, you can see the truth but can't see what to do or how to do much about it. It's as if you are looking at a closed box. You may be able to make an educated guess as to what is in the package by looking at the outside, but until you lift the lid and delve into its depths, you will never truly know what it contains, and therefore will never even really understand the purpose of the box.

If you remain outside, your perspective will be too limited. You must be willing to shift your vantage point by involving yourself with its inner world. Conversely, you may say it is similar to standing on a lower branch of a tree. The view of the landscape is limited by your current position, so you might be able to see trees and hear the sound of water, but you don't really know where you are in relation to the water and you can't know for sure what is going on with the water. Is it a rapid flowing river or a waterfall? Is it to the north or west of you? You can't be certain unless you climb higher up the tree, but once you climb high enough, you'll discover you're in a large forest with a meadow to your north and a small waterfall to the northwest.

Expanding your perspective allows you access to information which otherwise is simply not available. You can't know what is in the box until you open it. This act of opening shifts your relationship to the box. You can't see the forest through the trees unless you climb high enough to gain a perspective which permits a clearer view. Much of the work of self-transformation is merely gaining awareness. You can't change or even enjoy that which you cannot see and of which you are not aware. When you see something clearly enough, the energy to do something about it comes naturally. If you think you see something clearly but still can't seem to make a shift, I assure you there is still much that is eluding you.

When you see a bus rushing towards you, you move. If you can clearly see the ice is too thin, you don't step on it. The moment you actually stop making excuses and justifications for your drinking and see what a toll it is taking on your life, you seek help. The instant we openly acknowledge that your marital struggles are not changing by doing the same thing over and over again (if you wish to save it), you try to discover how to really change.

This book is designed to help *you*, the reader, understand the first three fundamental limited perspectives you hold as a human being (there are seven in all). The beauty of dealing with fundamentals is—once you've gained an expanded perspective on them—you'll find they universally apply throughout your life experience. This type of awareness is not limited to any one situation or circumstance but is applicable throughout all aspects of your life. It affects your relationships, your work, your home and, most importantly, on your inner world. Once you have a clear understanding of just one of these fundamental perspectives, you'll notice a shift in your perception on life. You'll have begun to peel away the vines that cover the *doors of perception*. Things will begin to feel less confusing, though paradoxically, more wonderfully mysterious. To experience life at this level of awareness is to begin to understand what it truly means to be human and opens a sense of purpose which previously escaped you.

These limited perspectives have thus far bound us as human beings to a confusing, restricted, inadequate interpretation of the world, and ourselves.

But no longer! This book is a call to arms. When you read the following pages, please know you are not only reading about how you can appreciate, expand and better understand yourself, but that you are learning how you can appreciate, expand and better understand the entire world. You are not separate from the world (the Second Perspective) but are an intricate, intimate part of the whole. So intricate, in fact, that the entirety of the world is known through you or not at all. You contain the foundation for a new world within your ability to become aware of the fact that, though you are not the world, you are not separate from the world, either!

To deeply understand this fact is to clear the clouds from the sky and feel the full radiance of the sun pouring over you so purely you can no longer distinguish the rays of light from the warmth of your skin because the waves have overtaken your desire to discriminate.

Limited Perspective 1

Our Six Senses

Your life experience is dominated by what you see, touch, hear, taste, smell and perhaps most of all, what you think. What if there is more to life? You feel so certain your day-to-day encounter with life is real. That how you see, touch, hear, taste, smell and think about the world is actually how it is.

Can you be so certain? History is riddled with examples which should cause you to seriously question such a rash assumption. To assume the way you perceive the world is objective is an immature belief akin to a child who believes in Santa Claus or the Tooth Fairy. Yet, if you pay close attention to how you go about your life, you will quickly discover your behavior proves you are still putting out cookies before midnight and hiding your baby teeth beneath a pillow, believing something magical is going to happen when you wake up. It is true something magical is happening, but you have to wake up from your childlike perspective first in order to find it. This starts with a deep recognition that life is far greater than your limited six senses can ever possibly perceive.

The Journey of the Mind

The journey of your mind and how thought has developed over the course of human history is quite possibly one of the most fascinating and illuminating subjects you can contemplate. The simplest way you may approach this daunting subject—and one which serves the purpose of this book—is to look at the development of thought through the lens of science.

Humans once had the perspective the earth was flat, the sun revolved around us and matter was solid, yet we now know none of these convincing assumptions proved to be true.

When we stood on the earth thousands of years ago and stared out at the sea, our six senses told us it was quite obvious that the earth we lived on and traversed was flat. Of course, there were hills, mountains and valleys but they all sat upon a flat surface much like the sea. This made perfect experiential sense, especially considering most of us didn't travel that far—and if we did, we eventually encountered a body of water which to all observing eyes looked as though it was flat and dropped off into oblivion at the horizon.

If humans stared up at the heavens, be it during the day or night, nothing could have been more obvious than the fact that the sun and stars spin around our planet. The notion that the earth is spinning at the rate of nearly 1,000 miles an hour would have seemed quite understandably absurd (that is, if we could even have conceived of a number and speed of that magnitude). The simplest and most logical rebuttal would have sounded something like, "That is ridiculous! If that were true, we would be thrown to the ground. It is impossible to stand still on something moving so fast. Look at me; do I look like I'm moving?! You're nuts!"

Then we have the issue of matter itself. This one may still prove challenging for most of us, even in our modern experience of the world. To comprehend that solid matter is 99.9999999999996% empty space is quite a stretch even for the most sophisticated among us, primarily because if we said something like that to someone holding a stick in their hand even a couple hundred years ago, they might respond by whacking us on the thigh followed by a comment something like, "Looks pretty solid to me, weirdo!"

The Dogma of our Six Senses

So, what does all this tell us? First, it quite explicitly displays that we should not be so cavalier about believing everything our six senses tell us, even though at this moment in time and space it may appear quite obvious and true. These are only three examples of literally hundreds where science has revealed over time that our senses are not as reliable as they may first seem.

Second, if we peer deeply into a direction science has been innocently and organically moving, we may discover there lies within it guidance for our human experience.

It is worth mentioning this direction is one which has been espoused by the deeper mystical aspects of religious and spiritual traditions spanning the breadth of recorded human history. Of course, their intentions and applications were quite distinct from that of science, but the fact that the path to greater awareness and deeper understanding share incredible similarities is quite remarkable and noteworthy.

What is this direction? It is the journey beyond your limited experience of the six senses. It is a slow stepping away from your myopic view of yourself and the world.

If we look carefully, we will recognize that we had to navigate past our common experience of the world to discover that the earth does not drop off at the horizon but instead curves back upon itself. In the past, we had to realize that quite literally, the universe does not revolve around us, even though our experience seems to indicate otherwise. Rather, we are just tiny specks in an immense cosmos. After that, we were faced with the fact that even something as solid and certain as objects themselves may have more mystery to them than appearance would dictate, and that the journey beyond ourselves does not only expand outward into space but proves equally as vast when turned inward.

If you pay close attention, you'll discover there is a dogma generated around your six senses, and even though this creed has been proven faulty and inadequate, you tend to cling to this belief. It is an understandable and even relevant loyalty at times to put all your trust and judgment into the hands of your six senses, but it proves eventually to be a problematic and even a dangerous bias.

If we never stepped beyond the limits of our five senses, all science would have stopped at the making of the wheel and hand tools. But through the sixth sense, our mind and the ability to conceptualize, think and rationalize, we've been able to transcend the confines of our five senses and discover dimensions which are really quite miraculous, even if they are ubiquitous.

Things such as electricity—an invisible force which powers much of your modern-day life—is a perfect example of your sixth sense's ability to transcend your five senses. Could there be more? Are you aware of all your capacities as a human and how to harness them? Most of what you use scientific development for is the fulfillment of your six senses, but this only displays a limited concept of your life and of yourself. When you take a good, hard look at how you apply knowledge and advancement, you'll quickly discover it is dominated by the gratification of primal pleasures which are determined only by considering your six senses. This would be fine and dandy if it proved sufficient in satisfying your desires, yet this is not the case.

The more you pursue physical pleasure, the farther away satisfaction appears to be. The more you get, the more you want, and the more you want, the more isolated and disconnected you feel. This is partly because the more things and experiences you acquire, the more complicated life becomes, and with this mounting complexity comes an overarching sense of burden. You then may turn to ideas such as voluntary simplicity or similar concepts, but again, you'll find no or limited peace here. This is because you have not recognized the problem accurately. If the world is only what your six senses tell you, you're held hostage by the limits to which they contain, and you inevitably find yourself isolated and confused by these limitations.

Why? Because your six senses predictably convince you the entire thing is a separate affair.

Limited Perspective 2

Separation

Your dependence and devotion to the six senses proves problematic for two primary reasons. One, it creates a myopic perspective of the world which is confined almost exclusively by *your* thoughts, feelings and desires. This is reinforced by the second problem, which stated clearly the *world*, including everyone and everything in it, stands outside of you. This seemingly obvious fact that we are separate beings is confirmed each time you look out your eyes, touch an object, hear a sound, smell a scent or taste drink or food. This basic experience of the world is what is commonly referred to as *subject* and *object*.

You are the subject of all your experiences, and that what you experience are the objects outside of you in the world. The separation of your inner world from the outer world is so fundamental to all your interpretations of what is happening in your life that you rarely, if ever, even consider this perspective may not be exactly as it appears. This assumed fact creates an extremely rigid and narrow perspective, one which rules almost all of your attention and decision-making. When you live solely from the sense that you are ultimately separate and unconnected to others and the objects around you, life begins to fade vaguely into a feeling of isolation. You then begin to seek ways to transcend this sense of smallness and separateness. You may go about this many different ways, but two of the most prevalent strategies are to seek pleasure as escape and/or to expand influence.

Avoidance

We find comfort in the pursuit of sense gratification. This comfort and pursuit only serves to distract us from the nagging sensation of loneliness and quickly begins to shift survival needs (i.e. food, shelter and clothing) into the realm of idolatry.

What do I mean by this? Well, the gratification of desire becomes your central focus and sole means for discovering any meaning or purpose in your life. But alas, you do not find any such reward there. Instead, as you quickly discover in modern times (which has crafted sense gratification into an art form that would make Michelangelo jealous), what you encounter is a deeper sense of isolation in the form of hopelessness. This hopelessness displays itself in a variety of ways, from nihilism, cynicism and fundamentalism of all sorts which is often experienced as a group, but manifests on the individual level through depression, anxiety, compulsive disorders and even ADHD. These symptoms (when deeply understood) are all clear indications that we're looking for answers in places where they'll never be found.

You may also attempt to avoid this powerful sense of aloneness and vulnerability by reaching for dominance over the outside world. This, too, can be done in a variety of ways, from seeking material success in the form of money and/or power (i.e. the consummate tycoon), to more subtle methods, such as dominating a spouse or coworker by tawdry, underhanded means—constantly talking, seeking attention or always needing to be right. The telltale sign of this behavior is its compulsive nature. When we can't stop working, planning, talking, judging or even "connecting," we can be certain we are doing this to avoid something. We are seeking to avoid the fact that we don't know what to do about this underlying feeling of exposure to the outside world and our subsequent loneliness and possible insignificance. The world is so vast, and we are so tiny. The objective realm is filled with so much which is unpredictable and potentially harmful. This little-liked fact dominates our next perspective.

Limited Perspective 3

Fear

When you're aware of nothing else but your six senses, you inevitably conclude you are separate from the outside world, and this sense of separateness unavoidably results in fear. The moment you accept that the world is outside of you, (if you watch closely) you will discover an immediate response of terror.

You are alone. You are exposed. There is no bridge to cross this moat between where you are and where the outside world exists. No matter how much you take into your vision, touch with your skin, expose your ears to, consume with your mouth and breathe in through your nostrils, you return to your side of the chasm, where you are forced to face the reality that you are always in, by yourself. This fact is never more starkly evident than in death. No matter how many family members and friends you have surrounding your deathbed, when that moment comes, you go alone. No one can accompany you in that crossover.

The Danger of the Sixth Sense

Your sixth sense (the mind) offers little help with this perspective, and in fact typically exacerbates the entire conundrum, because from the mind's perspective, there is so very much to be afraid of. You are so tiny in the face of such vastness. The physical world (where nothing is certain) cares very little about your personal plights. Danger in the form of physical, financial and emotional injury lurks around just about every corner, and when you include your loved ones in this circle of concern, it is a wonder you have time to do anything else but worry. The speed at which our current world moves and your exposure to endless amounts of information only proves to heighten your sense of vulnerability. Whether in the form of terrorism, common thievery, ecological deterioration, disease and ailments, political turmoil, cultural clashes and other disasters, we are overwhelmed with what is happening in our world and our sense of isolation and powerlessness can deepen as a result. The mind cannot conceive of how to ensure its survival, so it either attempts to ignore it all or it finds a few favorite issues on which to cling, which usually results in neurosis of one sort or another.

When the mind does attempt to deal with these deep existential issues, it often resorts to dogma, rituals and magical thinking. It attempts to decipher what it experiences in life so it can understand how to manipulate it to its benefit. Common examples are penances of all sorts, ritualistic prayers and/or mantras, affirmations, mechanical ceremony attendance, superstitions of all types, most Law of Attraction notions, astrology, many dietary methods and so on. It is fundamental to note that there is NOTHING wrong with any of these considerations, and indeed many—if not all—of them may be helpful, as long as you are not ascribing qualities and reasoning behind them which do not actually exist. The litmus test for discerning whether you are using these methods for manipulation as opposed to assistants in your journey of self-discovery is to watch closely to see if you are simply attempting to *avoid* your deep sense of fear and isolation through the use of these approaches.

This deep-rooted fear stemming from your sense of separateness which results from your stubborn assertion that all is encompassed by your six senses is at the very heart of humanity's confusion, struggles and suffering. You are tightly constrained by the limits of these three perspectives, and your adherence to their infallibility comes at a great price.

You lose touch with your sense of *Authentic Personal Power*, and in so doing, let go of the only means available for finding meaningful connection and genuine lasting contentment. This is your greatest loss. This is your fall from grace, your expulsion from the "Garden of Eden". The magnitude of this loss is worsened by the fact that most of us are not even aware of this departure. It is this sense of Self we are all desperately seeking and for which we internally yearn. Most of us have not awakened to this fact and so resort to replacing *Authentic Personal Power* with trite, cheap and damaging substitutes which come to full fruition in Perspective 4. It is vital to have a sense of direction if you ever hope to successfully navigate your way through your six senses, your sense of isolation and your deepest fears. *Authentic Personal Power* is the north star which can help guide you.

Before We Expand

It is important to state clearly and immediately that what you are about to explore as you expand your perspective may easily be sucked into the trap of the sixth sense—your mind. This is simply because I am using the only means by which I have to communicate, which is with the use of words, and yet words are by their very nature steeped deeply within the creation of your mind. To put this another way, and perhaps to state it more frankly, I am using words to attempt to express something, but you should be hyper-aware these words are not what I am actually talking about. If you allow this writing to become merely theoretical, you will lose the importance of the entire endeavor.

When I use a word like *Joy* or even words like *Authentic Personal Power*, it is crucial that you do not cling too tightly to any particular concept. If you are to experience what it is I am attempting to convey to you, you must be willing to actually *experiment* with it. Feel it. Open to it. Allow it to move within you. Search deep within yourself to see if you can discover for yourself the place to which I am pointing. If you are not willing to do this, you can expect no true insight into what is being conveyed. Instead, assume the reading of these words will simply be another distraction or form of escape that can then be used as yet another tool for avoidance. This is the last thing I wish to happen with this book.

To read this without the willingness to put it into action is like a person reading a recipe without actually ever being willing to cook anything and then expecting his or her stomach to be full. If you do not put this information into action through experimentation with deep curiosity and objectivity, you will never know if the recipe is any good. Even worse, if you do this for long enough, you'll die from starvation.

Expanding Perspective 1

"When you move beyond the six senses, you are leaving the gross world for the mystical, and here, everything is expressed in finer detail and with delicate nuance." - Adrien Fiorucci

The Dominant Sense

It shouldn't take long to recognize your five senses are largely, if not completely, dominated by your sixth sense. Perhaps an example will make this clearer. Let's look at a simple process—eating an apple. When you bite through its skin, you engage every one of your senses. You see the apple to pick it up, touch it as you place it in your mouth, hear the crunch as you take a nice big bite and smell and taste the apple as its juices and flesh enter your mouth. This quite sensuous event is filled with tremendous amounts of possible stimulation.

I use the word *possible* because too often this event can go by with little-to-no attention paid to it. How is this possible? It's a sensory extravaganza! Well, if you happen to be involved in a conversation or doing some other task such as looking at your device or lost in thinking about a past or future event, the experience will go largely unregistered (that is, unless the apple is especially enjoyable or unpleasant).

Why? How? Because you live predominantly within your sixth sense.

The dominance of your mind over the rest of your experiences place it front and center on the radar of what you should be considering as you attempt to understand how you might expand your perspective beyond the six senses. The straightforward fact that your mind filters all your other senses and then interprets how you think, feel and respond to all this stimulus dictates that you should begin here, with the mind. Start by acknowledging the fact that you are currently ruled by your sixth sense then you must have the courage to question what there is outside of the dictatorship you call thinking.

The Conundrum

The world is not what you think it is. At the same time, quite often *your* world is *only* what you think it is! Is there a bridge spanning this chasm between what the world is and what you think it is?

This is the primary question. The beauty of asking such a question is, if you inquire deeply enough, you'll begin to discover the enormity of your predicament, and with this, you will be stopped dead in your tracks. Similarly, when considering the vastness of the universe or the speed of light, you may be dumbfounded. In a certain way, all thinking stops because it cannot contain the immense nature of it. This type of experience may also occur in moments of great beauty, when the entire world slows down to show you a spectacular sunset, or when a physical gesture from someone you love falls delicately into your heart. It may also come in times of great sorrow or trauma, when the experience is too much for your mind to process and you are simply left with the raw happening. In that moment, there is nothing to make of it but what it is, more than the mind can encompass.

What happens when this occurs? When you have these types of experiences and thinking stops—what happens? Does the world end? Do you evaporate into nothingness? No. Yet if you are honest with yourself, it is very difficult for you to fathom what there is outside of thought.

Who are you without your thoughts, feelings and desires?

Oddly enough, upon later reflection, these types of experience may be held in high regard as times of great meaning, profundity and beauty, despite the fact that your mind was stumped at how to process them at first. In fact, it is precisely because your mind was quiet that you were able to purely encounter life as it is. When this occurs, there is a dawning of its innate beauty. Perhaps most surprisingly, this can happen even in times of tragedy or loss.

Understanding Your Five Senses

To venture beyond your six senses does not mean that you're attempting to remove them from your experience. Rather, it's quite the opposite. In order to go beyond, you must discover a willingness to delve inward. Perhaps this is what Heraclitus meant when he said almost 2,500 years ago, "The way up and the way down are one and the same." You do not transcend the senses by rejecting them, but by opening yourself fully to their intended purpose. The five senses are a portal to immediate presence and reflect the true nature of just about everything when the six sense (your mind) is given the proper perspective to view them.

What is this true nature? It is the temporary quality to all experience. Almost nothing stays still. Rather, everything is in a constant state of flux. Pleasure, pain, happiness, sorrow, success, failure, birth and death all are subject to impermanence. The five senses make this abundantly clear, if only you know how to look and take the time to do so. Instead, you've used these gifts to ardently avoid this unavoidable fact and you have done this at great harm to yourself, others and the world at large.

What is this proper perspective? If you look at your five senses from the common perspective, they appear as a tool to be used for self-gratification. Yet viewed from another angle, our five senses show you the quest for sense gratification results in fleeting events and cannot be sustained. The mere pursuit of pleasure and the compulsive avoidance of pain is a losing game.

How do you know this as fact? Because the more you acquire, consume or experience, the more you want to acquire, consume and experience. There is no lasting satisfaction found. Instead, there's an ever-increasing need for more. This sounds a lot like addiction, doesn't it? If you don't think you're addicted, it's a simple thing to check. The first thing you must do is recognize it, then STOP! Stop eating sweets for one week. Don't indulge in any technology or television for two weeks. Don't buy anything unnecessary for one month. These are only a few examples of things which you may find difficult to let go of and if you find yourself immediately saying, "I could do that." If you're uttering this phrase, then try it! And if you find yourself replying, "I *could* do it, but I don't *want* to do it. It's a stupid, pointless exercise," then you might want to look more closely at why you don't want to and not rush to the conclusion that it's because you think it is stupid.

Our Greatest Addiction

Your strongest addiction is not to consumerism, sex, alcohol, drugs or even the general pursuit of pleasure (even though this is a close second). Your greatest addiction is to thinking. Again, if you don't believe it, then stop. Anyone who has engaged in five minutes of meditation discovers almost immediately just how true this is. You are so addicted to thinking that you believe this is who you are. The Cartesian dictum *I think, therefore I am* states this notion clearly and perhaps accounts for its popularity. Whatever thoughts pop into your mind you assume and then assimilate as you.

What else could they be? They did appear in your mind and not someone else's, right? True, but this does not necessarily make them yours. It is easy to realize that not all thoughts are yours when someone makes an outlandish statement and you take a moment to *think* about it but then quickly and easily dismiss it as ridiculous. However, you have trouble dismissing thoughts which we feel are original (even when quite often they are equally as ridiculous).

This may be difficult to hear and even a bit disconcerting, so brace yourself, but repetition more than anything else accounts for your sense of self. The famous quote from Joseph Goebbels, "If you repeat a lie often enough, it becomes truth," may have just as much relevance here as it does in politics. Just because you have had a thought and then repeated it dozens, perhaps hundreds or (heaven forbid) even thousands of times does not make it true or who you are. Perhaps it may be more accurate to say this thought or identity has no fundamental claim on who you are. Under the right circumstances with the proper motivation and a certain degree of awareness and clarity, you can give up any thought or preconceived notion of who you think you are. Even if you have thought it a thousand times and believed it was unquestionably true.

This repetition is a form of addiction and this form of addiction is the cause of just about all neurosis such as depression, anxiety, compulsion and much more. The use of repetition can be used for more positive results. We see this rampant in the motivational and self-empowerment movements which have become very popular in the past 50 years. This is indeed a constructive use of the reality of repetition, but it falls short in two important and fundamental ways.

Thought is not Reality

The self-empowerment movement rarely acknowledges the fact that:
1) Thought is not reality and
2) The pursuit of happiness is not significantly different from the pursuit of pleasure, especially if it is still motivated by and secretly centered around the avoidance of pain.

The fact is, no matter which thoughts you cultivate in your mind, they are not reality. To put this simply and not get too philosophical, the word apple is NOT the apple and no matter how much you think about an apple, it will not fill your tummy, nor will thinking about picking an apple from a tree actually pluck it from its resident stem.

Why? Because thought, while powerful, useful and miraculous is NOT reality. Thought *influences* your reality, but you should not mistake this fact for the belief that thought *is* reality. This is the first point that is often missed or misunderstood when it comes to self-empowerment. As you begin to understand the nature of mind and the immense impact it has on reality, you can quickly get carried away with this realization. What typically occurs is an awakening from unconscious thinking and then a full-on embrace of what might be considered conscious thinking. Again, this is a fundamental step forward but should not be mistaken for a final destination or even the purpose of thought. This would be like believing the sail on a sailboat is responsible for sailing, when in fact it is the wind that moves it and the ocean that supports the structure. The sail has its place and is instrumental in *how* the boat moves through the water but it should NOT be mistaken for the wind or the sea.

Happiness is Not Joy

As for the second point, if you look closely, you might discover the impulse behind the desire to move your thinking from unconscious to conscious comes from a place within yourself that is not significantly different from where you began. This is to say that you attempt to manipulate thinking by a similar use of repetition. This is the same method which got you where you are in the first place. Though this alone may be enough to give you pause, it is not the central flaw in this approach. The motivation behind *why* you are choosing to do this is the principle error, and in a fundamental way may leave you unchanged more than it first might appear. Simply put, you are again merely attempting to avoid pain and pursue pleasure.

Is there nothing more to a human being than this? Surely there is! However, you may never discover it without understanding this as the fundamental drive of the six senses. When you begin to see, deeply see, that we as humans do almost nothing but avoid pain and pursue pleasure, you can start to consider what else there is.

Much of this longing to feel pleasure you'll begin to attribute to a sense of happiness. You assume, somewhat logically, that because happiness feels so good, this must be the meaning to life. There are many spiritual-sounding teachers and practices which espouse this exact point—that because happiness feels good, it is an indicator that it is your innate nature calling you to pursue it. They also note that you are a better human being when you are happy. This seems all the more to support such a belief that the pursuit of happiness is the goal to life. But there is something very important and essential which is missed. Happiness is NOT Joy. This may seem like splitting hairs, but the nuance of the difference is critical to understand and is too often not clearly enough expressed.

Happiness is a fleeting thing and pursuing it as an end goal is futile and can only lead to frustration or shallowness. Joy, on the other hand, *is* your fundamental nature and does not shift, nor is it dependent upon any condition or prerequisite. Joy does not care if you have money. It does not need to travel or have incredible life-affirming experiences. It simply *is* and waits for you to recognize it everywhere and in everything. Joy is present in the catastrophic loss as much as it is in the birth of a healthy newborn baby. Joy is what awaits you beyond the six senses, because it is not subject to them, even though it can be experienced with them.

This subtle difference is like mistaking west on the compass for southwest. As you first begin your journey by following your compass, you will not notice a great deviation and all will seem well. But given enough time, you'll eventually become lost and will not arrive at your intended destination.

In the spiritual life, subtlety is everything and it must be paid concise attention. When you move beyond the six senses, you are leaving the gross world for the mystical, and here, everything is expressed in finer detail and with delicate nuance.

This is where the vibrancy and vitality of living lies, but you have been too busy paying attention to the superficial aspects of life which have left your observation skills dull and clumsy. Experiencing the difference between happiness and Joy is like walking out of a room lit with a single lightbulb into the radiance of a cloudless summer sky at noon. Understanding that you are more than your six senses is akin to opening the door from this room. All that remains is that you learn how to walk through to understand the power and significance of the sun.

Contemplation for Expanding Perspective 1

As the world performs
its glorious play of charm and dread
I'm not compelled to engage.

There is something within
that commands my attention
that pulls me deep into another world.

This world
is neither defined nor confined
by my six senses

(although they are part of it)
but rather calls me
to its innermost being

I have been invited
to appreciate
the heart of mystery.

A sincere exploration
of the internal nature
of all things.

I ask,
what, where and who
is this?

I cannot know!
But maybe
I feel it every day.

In fact,
I'm experiencing it
right this second!

But I trivialize it
through the limits
of my six senses,

cheapen it
by measuring its worth
with how much pleasure

I can extract,
like weighing
the beauty of a flower

against how long it may bloom.
This sin
misses the mark.

Seeing Beyond

In order that I may
let the grandeur
of a blossom

into my heart,
I must let go
of who I think I am

and become the flower
and let the flower
become me.

Only then can I know its colorful secrets
only then will I taste its challenges
that pulled this bud from the earth

and stretched its stem
to the heavens,
reaching out beyond the limits

of its need to know
by simply being
blossoming dying

so that
it may be
born again

Exercises for Expanding Perspective 1

-1-

At least once every day for a week, take the time to envision yourself on a sailboat drifting out at sea on a beautiful sunny afternoon. A steady but gentle breeze is at your back and the world is at ease. Feel the current of life leading you in a direction beyond your petty personal desires and open your sails to receive the guidance and power of the wind. Imagine you are holding the rudder gently in your hand, not trying to force any particular direction but instead aligning yourself with the naturally-existing currents of life. Feel the soothing, tender rocking of the water as it completely holds and supports you. Take a deep breath of the ocean-fresh air and breath it out slowly, knowing you are part of something greater than you could ever imagine. All is well. In fact, it is exactly as it ought to be!

-2-

Choose one thing that you really enjoy and decide to go without it for five days. Whether it is a cup of coffee, sweets, television, social media, the news, etc. and make this choice with the full intention that you are engaging in a grand experiment. You are investigating just how attached you are to this particular thing. With curiosity, watch how your six senses react and behave. Notice what happens and how they respond to an injection of willpower. You may want to journal the whole thing as a way to monitor what is happening and to access greater clarity. Remember you are researching the question: Is there more to me than my six senses? Who is it that makes this choice to refrain? Who is it that wants to call the whole thing stupid and quit? Remember every time you confront the urge to indulge and resist you are building an inner muscle, and much like a physical muscle, it burns a little when it's worked out. So, if you are not experiencing an inner burn, you may want to choose something else you care more about to create an environment of mild resistance.

-3-

Seeing Beyond

Meditate for 15 -20 minutes every day for a week. Do this meditation with your eyes open. Sit comfortably in a quiet place with your back straight and hands resting effortlessly in your lap. Take three conscious deep breaths, noticing how your chest expands and contracts, observe how the body moves with the breathing and how the spine extends and settles ever so slightly with the ribcage. Settle into your body with no sense of duty or obligation. You are simply sitting here relaxing with your eyes open. Take the first thing your eyes land on and look at it closely. Take in its shape and color and sit with that for a minute. Then ask yourself, who looks through these eyes? Who is doing the seeing? Don't attempt to answer the question. Instead, simply sit with it. After a few moments, pay attention to the first sound you hear and ponder who is it that hears this sound. Ask yourself, how do I know who hears this and how can I tell from where this sound arises? Again, you are not as interested in the answer as much as the act of innermost searching. This, too, is building an inner muscle, and this muscle is strengthened by holding fast to not knowing. Notice the sensation of your clothing on the surface of your skin and see if you can focus in on the outermost edge of you. Where do you end and the clothing begin? Do you have access to this exact point? How? Before you get up, take three more conscious breaths. Allow the in breath to expand the sense of your physical body. Feel it grow with the filling of air making you as large as your body permits. Now gently release the air and feel your body shrink and imagine you are letting go of something unnecessary, something you have been carrying for a long time.

Expanding Perspective 2

> *"A human being is a part of the whole that we call the universe, a part limited in time and space. He experiences himself, his thoughts and feelings, as something separated from the rest—a kind of optical illusion of his consciousness. This illusion is a prison for us, restricting us to our personal desires and to the affection for only the few people nearest us. Our task must be to free ourselves from this prison by widening our circle of compassion to embrace all living beings and all of nature."* -Albert Einstein

Separation (The Way Out is In)

This "illusion"—as Einstein refers to it—is set into motion by our dogged belief that the universe is only our six senses and if we wish to free ourselves from this "prison" we must understand how we got here in the first place. As we have already noted from Heraclitus, much of what it takes to free ourselves from the prison of the six senses is counterintuitive, which may account for the fact that most of us go through our entire lives without even considering such a thing. Because you have unconsciously accepted the limits of your six senses, you are ruled by their inadequate assessment of experience. How to gain compassion—as Einstein so wisely suggests—and have an intimate sense of connection with all living creatures and nature is the imperative question. One of the most misinterpreted and powerful tools available to us for just such a task is *Vulnerability*. It is so easily missed because when the six senses run into vulnerability, we immediately translate this experience as dangerous. Feeling vulnerable to the six senses is to feel weak, exposed, to be defenseless, frail and ill-prepared, but as you shall see, nothing could be further from the truth.

Vulnerability and Authentic Personal Power

The relation between vulnerability and *Authentic Personal Power* may at first be difficult to understand, but they are inextricably linked. You will only allow vulnerability when you have some sense of *Authentic Personal Power* and yet paradoxically, you can only grow into your *Authentic Personal Power* through the experience of vulnerability. These two things are intimately connected. When you stand in a sense of your own *Authentic Personal Power*, you are not as intimidated by the uncomfortable feelings associated with vulnerability. You know you are up to the challenge and the belief of your frailty is removed, which then unlocks the ability to see the benefits of this experience. Your six senses mistook the uncomfortable quality of vulnerability as a sign that it is bad, but this is a hasty conclusion and one which has led to a great deal of confusion and struggle.

Let's take a moment to review that the overarching perception of Perspective 2 is that the world is a separate affair. When you believe this, it is hard to see vulnerability any other way but as a potentially harmful exposure to the outside world. This assumption creates certain inevitable emotions and reactions. When you feel insecure, you seek ways to protect yourself. You usually do this in the form of building walls. These walls—or boundaries—may have many different appearances, but let's consider three of the most common ones. Now imagine these as fences see if they seem familiar to you, either as people you know or, more importantly, as personal ways you might be avoiding vulnerability. The three biggies are as follows: the barbed-wire fence, the white-picket fence and the invisible fence.

The Barbed Wire Fence

This boundary usually presents itself as some show of force. This force can come in the form of actual aggression, such as someone who always pushes their viewpoint, opinion or seeks to always get their way, but another very common display is the person who can never be quiet. They may not be pushing any particular view or opinion, but they cannot allow a moment of silence and they are incapable of actually listening. They do this as a way of controlling their interactions with people and they feel the compulsion to do this because they are terrified of what the other might say if they are given the chance.

Many of these people appear to have great confidence and may even seem quite genuine until you have spent a sufficient amount of time with them. The use of force can never be fully maintained simply because it requires too much effort. If you are present during an unguarded moment with these people, you'll quickly see behind the barbed-wire fence witnessing that they are nothing like the image they are so tirelessly portraying. In fact, they are almost always the exact opposite!

It is important to point out that force should never be confused with power. They are two very different things, even though they are often mistaken as the same. Force comes from a place of lack and is an overcompensation for that perceived deficiency, whereas Power comes from a position of abundance and feels no need to push or compensate for anything. (This will be elaborated upon in Perspectives 4.)

The White Picket Fence

This boundary is busy presenting itself as the perfect solution for all problems. It is concerned with appearing to be agreeable, liked and having it all together. In a certain way, it is hard to see this as a wall against vulnerability because many of these people appear so approachable and pleasant. Yet a closer examination of the fence and we see it is rotten. It is only their constant application of white paint which makes it appear healthy. These people busy themselves with appearance and pleasantries because deep down they are frightened that if anyone knew who they really were, they would be rejected, ridiculed and inevitably find themselves alone (the worst of all nightmares).

One of the telltale signs of this boundary is that these people hate to be alone. They fill their schedules with activities which require them to constantly be on the go. Conversely, they may be a person who has attached themselves to one or two people, requiring their continuous validation by being in constant contact with them. Again, this appears to be an act of engagement which does bear a close resemblance to vulnerability but differs greatly because of the intent which lay behind the interactions and their typical shallow exchange. Vulnerability is not something we can experience on the fly. You can't cram in five minutes for vulnerability and then move on. Vulnerability requires that you take the time to respect the fact you are being vulnerable. In this way, you can clearly see this is not what the person who builds white picket fences is interested in at all. They are occupied with creating the appearance of connection without ever having to experience it beyond their comfort level.

Why? Because there is a hidden belief that if they venture beyond their fence, something will get trampled and broken. They do not feel capable of dealing with this, so it's best to avoid the entire thing. They feel this way because they do not have a sense of their *Authentic Personal Power*.

The Invisible Fence

This boundary is very clever in that it does not show itself at all. You might also call this the silent fence in that people who exhibit this behavior pattern tend to be very quiet. The consummate introvert fits this model quite well. They avoid vulnerability by staying out of the line of fire. They do their best to fade into the background. They typically are great listeners and use this skill to keep the center of focus on anyone or anything else but themselves. They are more comfortable being alone than with other people and therefore spend lots of time by themselves. They tend to be intelligent and gifted people, but this usually remains a secret kept even from themselves.

Why would an individual who is so gifted and intelligent choose to hole up in their room alone? Because they do not have a sense of their *Authentic Personal Power* and unfortunately, they are unlikely to discover it within the confines of the four walls of their favorite hiding space.

With this type, it is easier to see that they avoid interaction, confrontation and exploration because they feel frail, as if just about anything could break them. They are meek individuals who have accustomed themselves to demanding very little from others, in the hope that not much will be asked of them. They do this because deep inside, they feel weak, incapable or insufficient.

What is ironic and may even be quite astonishing to many readers is this feeling is shared by all three types. The lack of connection with *Authentic Personal Power* is the root cause, though it may manifest itself in starkly different ways.

Note: It's important to point out these are types which should never be taken too literally. They are generalizations, and as such, are painted with a very wide brush stroke. A person who fits the invisible fence metaphor may have a place in their life where they indeed do feel quite powerful, just as the barbed wire fence individual may have a fairly apparent place of weakness which seems uncharacteristic of them.

The Willingness to be Vulnerable

What does vulnerability and *Authentic Personal Power* have to do with our deep sense of isolation and separateness? In order that you might begin to bridge the gap between your belief that the world is outside of you, you must be *willing* to experience life as it is. You must be willing to let down your guard and open yourself up to what is right before your eyes. In the words of Jesus, "Having eyes do you not see, and having ears do you not hear?" Unfortunately, the answer is a resounding NO. A major part of why you do not "see" is because you are not *willing* to see. You are not willing to be vulnerable. Being willing to be vulnerable opens you by taking down these fences, which allows you to set down the veil you have placed between you and what you perceive as the outside world. This shroud is responsible for the illusion that there is separation at all. When you become willing to lift this veil, you'll experience vulnerability, and this, in turn, unlocks the portal to new experiences of *Authentic Personal Power*. Vulnerability on its own does NOT do this, but *the willingness to be vulnerable* does!

Typically, we as human beings do not embrace this, but instead run away from vulnerability and build walls/fences to prevent it. Why? Because we are afraid of what might happen. Because being vulnerable is full of uncertainty. We cannot predict the outcome and therefore are not sure if we are up for the challenge. To be vulnerable is to be open and alive!

This is only a problem when you do not have a deep sense of your *Authentic Personal Power*. Much of this sense of lack stems ironically from your unwillingness to experience vulnerability. To be vulnerable is indeed to be open, but open does not necessarily mean defenseless, and it certainly does not mean powerless. Being willing to face the uncertainty of vulnerability is not an act of weakness, but rather a tremendous display of courage. And whenever you exercise this type of will, you harness the very power of creation!

Adrien Fiorucci

Seeing through an Illusion

It is important to pay close attention to the fact that all your boundaries and efforts to control reality by limiting your exposure to vulnerability will never protect you completely from the uncertainties of life. It is an illusion. Sickness still occurs, loss of possessions and loved ones is inevitable, embarrassment and even failure is unavoidable, and you may squander incredible amounts of energy on attempting to ward off what is inescapable. What is worse is every time you do this; you do not strengthen yourself. On the contrary, you weaken your ability to deal with life as it is, and this fact is the source of your disconnection with *Authentic Personal Power*.

It is similar to the proverbial "helicopter mom" who tries to protect her child from all dangers, including emotional turmoil and discomfort. By doing this, she inhibits her child's inner learning and growth, because she does not allow the child to work through his or her own problems. By doing this, she never allows the child to attain a sense of ownership with a solution. This sense of ownership awakens within the child a recognition of his or her own ability to handle whatever life has to offer and builds confidence and an appreciation that the child can get through whatever life might deliver, whether it is painful or not. The famous quote from Winston Churchill rings true here; "Success is not final. Failure is not fatal: it is the courage to continue that counts."

It is also critical to realize that when you rely on boundaries to protect you from vulnerability, you are filtering out some of the most precious and delicious aspects of life. You will never know deep, intimate connection without potential exposure to emotional harm or disappointment. Once you discover disappointment and emotions are not fatal, you can begin to open yourself to the rich, meaningful and even profound interactions which await you on the other side.

The Revelation of Vulnerability

By slowly developing a willingness to risk the uncomfortable sensations of vulnerability, you begin to penetrate through the illusion of separation. This is because the more you experience intimate connection, the more apparent it becomes that all distance and division occurs solely in your mind. It is your sixth sense (the mind) which creates this interpretation of reality, and it is your mind which has created the elaborate framework in which to deal with this misinterpretation.

This behavior is similar to a man who sees a snake in his basement and then begins to construct barriers and obstructions to keep the snake confined to its dark corner. He then starts to plot ways in which he might rid himself of this threatening pest. After much deliberation and searching, the best he can come up with is a shovel. With the shovel in one hand, he grabs his flashlight with the other, and steadies his nerves as he approaches the barricades he had so hastily assembled earlier. Much to his surprise and wonder, he discovers with the illumination from his light that the snake was simply a rope all along.

Through the repeated experience of being willing to feel vulnerability in a relatively safe environment, you accustom yourself to the odd and quite often unpleasant sensations which accompany it. As you do this, you begin to rewire the brain to stop associating vulnerability with things like weakness and danger. Instead your brain starts to understand on a visceral level that there is much to be gained from a willingness to risk and endure the initial uneasy feelings of vulnerability. You begin to recognize that within you there is a place of power.

Authentic Personal Power dwells within each of us, waiting patiently as we find our way through the surface of experience into the deeper dimensions of what is truly going on. The remarkable yet inevitable discovery is to recognize who you truly are, a being of boundless abilities and unlimited sensitivities. What you learn as you build *Authentic Personal Power* is vulnerability is a heightened state of awareness. Similar to the fight-or-flight response, where your senses become acute as a way of preparing you for quick reactions to either defend or run, vulnerability heightens your senses so you may deeply experience a feeling of awareness of the world and yourself. When you have a sufficient appreciation for your *Authentic Personal Power*, you can willingly open yourself further to these intimate encounters and discover another dimension to life that is lush, precious and so utterly remarkable that it is baffling you should have ever chosen to ignore or avoid it.

The Inspiration of Vulnerability

Another remarkable benefit which naturally occurs when you authentically and willingly act in a vulnerable way is you inspire others to do the same. You give permission to the rest of the world to display their potential and offer up the gift of what they might otherwise be keeping tucked away. This may not happen immediately, but it will occur if you do not falter in your fidelity to this higher calling.

Think about it—when someone is authentically vulnerable with you, do you think of them as weak and pathetic? Probably not. You most likely find it inspiring. You may even find yourself caught up in the moment, sharing something you might otherwise not have.

This is because to be vulnerable is not an act of weakness but an act of inner strength and courage, and these two attributes are stimulating and contagious. When you engage in interactions like these, you encounter intimacy, and these types of exchanges and relationships are the ones which stand out.

Why? Because they break through what would otherwise be mundane and confined. This monotony and restriction are created by your constant effort to protect yourself from harm. However, this type of intimacy can happen anywhere, whether it is in the lobby waiting for an appointment or at the dinner table with your child or spouse. If you do not venture into vulnerability, you can expect either silence or dullness from these situations. But if you are willing to take the chance, you will discover willing cohorts, and your experience of life will become richer and more fulfilling because of it.

Please note this is not some attempt to turn introverts into extroverts, nor is it a license for the extrovert to ramp up his or her already potentially overbearing presence. This should be considered by degree and depth, which is to say, if you are a naturally quiet soul, perhaps you might venture out a bit more, especially with those to whom you feel closest. If you are the outgoing type, perhaps you might pay closer attention to what you are putting out and consider if it might contain a little more substance or intimacy. It isn't about how much you say, or even what you share, but how you say and share it. The place you are coming from when you interact with another human being will determine its quality and effect.

Vulnerability is unique to each individual, so what makes an introvert feel vulnerable will quite often be very different from that of an extrovert. A stark example of this would be that for the extrovert, being quiet may be the greatest act of vulnerability, which then gives the introvert his or her opportunity to grow and shine!

Entering a New Dimension

By developing a willingness to experience vulnerability, you transform vulnerability into a portal which opens up within you new dimensions. What results when you enter into this new way of experiencing the world is a radical shift of perspective. As you begin to have deep, intimate connections with the world "outside" of you, you will discover the distance between "us and them" is not so great after all.

When you have a tender, innocent moment with a child, or silently watch a sunset over moving water, or with your whole body breathe in the smell of fresh cut grass—if you pay close attention—you'll notice that at that moment there is no separation. The moment the child smiles and your heart opens to it, you smile back, and there is only openness and smiling and, in that exchange, there is connection. There is union. There is no separation. When you feel the beauty of the colors which spread over the sky and dance as reflections on the water, you experience this dance, these reflections, within your very soul, and there is only this moment. There is no separation. When you open your senses to the familiar, pungent green odor of exposed grass, you immediately become grounded by memories which run so deep they almost appear eternal; you realize you stand here not only *on* the grass, but *as* the grass in that this powerful aroma is itself the grass entering into you. Instead of believing anything I am saying, pay close attention—it's happening right now!

Though these moments may be fleeting at first, they are a clear signal that there is more going on than you commonly pay attention to, and just because they may come and go does not mean they are not real, or that they are somehow relegated to uncommon phenomenon. The fact is, this is always occurring. You simply do not take the time to notice it and have not yet developed the skill to expand your limited perspective. This perspective that tells you that you're separate because you have these six senses that register what is going on in the world. To think that this makes you separate would be like saying a leaf is separate from the tree because it has senses which take in the sunlight. You are not separate from life because you experience it. You are an intricate, intimate part of life because you experience it. You are life experiencing itself!

Contemplation for Expanding Perspective 2

The wonder of this world
is not a mystery which cracks
under the weight of our senses

but is magnified
by them.

This is because
we can contemplate

because *how* and *why*
unlocks things
that are often kept secret
from the eyes and ears
of common experience.

This does not diminish mystery,
it amplifies it.

The connection
to all things
hidden and seen
balance on our willingness
to open to it
to encounter it
As It Is.

To open
to this mystery
is to invite the unknown
into our eyes, ears,
noses, mouths, skins
and minds

This summons
the previously untapped Power
of our beings.

This great reservoir
holds all things
in its boundless banks

including our souls,
innermost longing,
most precious wish,
and most furtive desire
to *belong*.

To know that we are known—
and to feel the roots
of who we are
reaching deep

into the depths
of what it means to be alive—

We must remember
the Power which causes
the stars to burn
is born in us.

The very air that we breathe
was birthed from the elements
that reach all the way back
to the dawn of time.

Indeed,
this is our legacy and home,
even the galaxies
are held within our cells.

To claim this inheritance
is to rejoice
at the mystery
of how it
and we
got here at all!

Exercises for Expanding Perspective 2

-1-

Quite often, a good way to experience vulnerability in a palpable way is to have an experience of deep connection with something you may consider to be inanimate. It is best to start with something simple and benign, such as a flower, a favorite stone or even a candle flame. Sit quietly with this object for three minutes or more. Start with a few deep breaths to ground yourself and see if you can relax into your body. Loosen your shoulders and back muscles and just look at the object. Take it in and open yourself to it. Look not only with your eyes but with your entire body. Notice details you overlooked at first glance and see if you can't sense an energetic quality to it which is almost akin to a personality. That is to say, this object is unique from all other objects in the entire universe. Nowhere else is this object present but right here and right now before you. Can you appreciate the miracle of that? Can you sense the eternally shifting nature of it? This object will not remain like this, and in fact is changing right before your eyes, even if you cannot perceive it—just as you yourself are changing as you gaze upon it. Stay present with your whole body as you both interact. You share this space and time together. Can you feel this? You will not feel it unless you open yourself to it. Unless you become vulnerable to the presence of this object, you will not be able to sense what I am trying to point out. But if you do open, if you do make yourself vulnerable, you will immediately experience an intimacy with the object which was hidden from you before. This intimacy is a breaking down of the barrier which once was your belief that indeed you are separate from this object. This is the beginning of a whole new dimension to living.

-2-

Take one day of the week for a month (preferably the same day, such as Sundays, for example) and dedicate time to your senses. Do this by taking a walk in nature (barefoot if possible, even for a short time) and take note of the sensation of the earth on the underside of your feet. If you are wearing shoes, simply imagine you are barefoot and attempt to really feel the earth and its texture beneath you as it reaches up to support your every step. Take note of any odors being carried enigmatically through the air. See if you can notice all the points on your skin that meet the breeze as it pauses for a moment to make contact with you before it continues its journey across the globe. Detect the different sounds all around you, be they the leaves rustling as they dance or birds singing their perpetual song of motion and intrigue. After you have taken this walking meditation on being present with Mother Nature, draw yourself a bath. In this bath, be sure to include some form of aroma therapy, such as scented Epsom salts or essential oils in a diffuser. Light a candle (which may also be your source of scent) and enter the sanctuary of the water. (If you do not have a bathtub, then take a long, warm shower.) Pay special attention to the sensation of the water on your skin and the sounds that are made from your movement and interaction with it. Make yourself vulnerable to this special moment of indulgence by breathing deep and relaxing into the fact that you needn't do anything but simply be here right now in the simplest way you know how. Everything is right, because you can do nothing wrong in this moment as you notice the scent filling your bathroom with a sense of ease and enchantment. Take a moment when you feel especially vulnerable and connected to realize you are this moment. By taking the time to enjoy this precise moment, you are participating in an act of pure gratitude. Be grateful from the tips of your hair follicles to the very bottom of your feet and know you are cared for. Now inquire deep within yourself…who had all these experiences, and did you need any of them to be who you are? Don't try to answer the question. Simply sit with it…

-3-

Meditate for 15-20 minutes every day for a week. Sit comfortably in a quiet place with your back straight and hands resting effortlessly in your lap. Close your eyes and take three conscious deep breaths. Notice how your body feels as it begins to find rest in this moment. Is there tension? If so, notice where and intend to let it go a little more with each breath. See if you can't find a moment of solace in your body by simply being here in an uncomplicated and abandoned manner. Relax your facial muscles and open your jaw very slightly to help keep your facial muscles loose. Take a moment to fully inhabit your body. By this I mean, see if you can't find the outermost part of your body. Where does your skin meet your surroundings? Can you feel it? The surface you are sitting on—can you feel its support? Explore the outermost reaches of your legs, your feet, your arms, your hands, and then ever so gently and slowly begin to pull yourself in. Slowly, tenderly draw your awareness inward toward your heart as if you were calling all the parts of yourself to the safety and warmth of home. This heart is your home. Rest here for the remainder of the meditation, simply breathing into your heart center. When thoughts arise, notice you have been caught by them and gently offer them to your heart center, which is always willing to accept and receive. One breath at a time, one thought at a time, you gradually enter deeper into your heart, the center of all connection, vulnerability and Power.

Expanding Perspective 3

Fear

Fear is quite possibly the single most influential human emotion. This is because fear is so fundamental to how we perceive the world and our self in it. Once you believe you are hostage to your six senses in the world outside, your sensing becomes isolated from you. Once you feel this isolation, you are likely to experience fear. To be alone is perhaps one of the most common and gripping of our fears, which is witnessed by all our attempts to avoid it. A close relative to isolation or separateness is the unknown. You fear the unknown in all its forms, which ironically takes the shape of your underlying condition as a human being. To be human is to live with the fear of uncertainty, not because you know so little, but because you *think* you should "know" so very much.

Isn't it true that none of us actually know what is going to happen today when we step outside the confines of our homes, or if the person driving 60 mph next to us on the expressway is going to behave rationally and stay in their lane, or if we will wake up in the morning once again after we fall asleep tonight? The list extends further than that. This is the setting in which we find ourselves, thrust deep into the heart of the unknown and this terrifies us…but only when we think we should know.

Knowing We Don't Know

"It's not what you don't know that kills you, it's what you know for sure that ain't true." Mark Twain

This quote says a lot about the human experience and much of what I am trying to illuminate here. To think you *should* know causes the anxiety about the fact that you simply cannot know. Nowhere does Mark Twain's quote ring truer than in the realm of science. The history of scientific discovery is riddled with significant moments which has laid waste to something we'd held as fact for centuries. Think back to the beginning of the book to highlight just a tiny portion of these events. The irony is that science is the pursuit of knowledge, which is to say, our attempt to end this suffering of uncertainty by striving to know the unknown. Yet again and again, we discover we must reevaluate our findings.

Seeing Beyond

Does this mean it is a futile attempt, a waste of time? No, of course not. But to believe you can think your way out of this conundrum is likely to lead you to further confusion and despair.

Why? Because thinking is what got you here in the first place. That statement is not meant to disparage thinking, but only to clarify its role and limits. If you are to make peace with the uncertainty which will almost certainly be here for the foreseeable future, you must get in touch with something else. Something of a higher order. Something which stands outside of— while at the same time resides deep within— your condition as a human.

If you are terrified when you take a good earnest look at the precarious situation in which you find yourself, it's because you reason it should be different. But the simple, obvious fact is, that it is not, nor has it ever been different.

The reality that we cannot predict the future and how events will unfold has been with us from the dawn of time. To take this one step further into the direction of expanding this perspective, we do not, nor can we, even control our bodies in a fundamental way. This is to say, we do not breath our lungs, they do so on their own. We do not pump our blood by thinking our heart into compliance, it does so on its own. Our liver, kidneys and thyroid (the list goes on) function, or don't, without our conscious doing. In fact, if we were to be forced to try to function our thyroid with our conscious thought, we would be at a complete loss as to how to do so.

The point here is even our bodies (which we take to be our very own) have a destiny of their own which in large part we are incapable of controlling.

How does this get you any closer to feeling better about fear? How is this expanding this perspective? If you pay close attention to this, it is much like a rollercoaster ride. Some people love rollercoasters and some people hate them.

Throughout the history of humanity, the condition just described has been with us. Throughout this long and varied history some people have thrived in it and others, not so much. Some people have mastered this perspective so thoroughly that they thrived not in *spite* of fear and uncertainty, but because of it. How?

Authentic Personal Power

Much like the fact that you do not beat your heart or breath your lungs, *you* cannot thrive in fear and uncertainty. But thankfully, *you* do not have to. Something else has already taken care of this for you. You simply need to get in touch with this reality. To discover *Authentic Personal Power* is to get in touch with the very core of your Self and all things. This is the Power which resides in the act of your lungs breathing on their own. I am not talking about the medulla, but the source which originated such a marvelous creation as the human brain in the first place. The Power which sustains it right now in this very moment. To try to quantify what this Power is would probably be naïve, but to deny that such a Power exists or to chalk it up to coincidence or chaos would be a far more naïve notion. You don't need to label it or pin it down with dogma to get in touch with its nature and utilize its limitless potential any more than water needs to understand geology or be a physicist in order to flow through the earth and create a waterfall.

There is nothing wrong with attempting to understand what *Authentic Personal Power* is. Indeed, that is what we are doing here. But you will never truly understand it by only thinking about it. You must involve yourself in the conscious act of understanding how you are already experiencing it all the time. This is the purpose in pointing out that so much of what you consider "your" body operates quite independently from your conscious mind. This is most certainly why working with the breath is part of every major religion.

Why? Because it is a physical happening which can portal you into the ineffable when you pay close attention to it. First, the act of breathing happens on its own, yet at the same time you *can* consciously choose to participate in this act and alter your breathing. Second, when you pay close attention, breathing is a continuous act of intimacy and exchange. You are constantly taking in the "outside" world into the very cells of your body and releasing a part of yourself to this same "outside." Inevitably, this type of profundity could be said with just about everything, but the immediacy your breath offers makes it a wonderful place to start to realize just how real this is.

Suffering and Inauthenticity

Once you begin a genuine, meaningful relationship with *Authentic Personal Power,* you begin to recognize it cannot be pigeonholed—it is best to allow it to be what it is at the moment you stumble upon it. The moment you attempt to capture it with thought, desire or emotion, you immediately limit it. This limitation is not in alignment with its limitless nature. You then run the risk of losing what it really is by hyper-focusing on a few aspects of what you *think* it is, or worse yet, what you *want* it to be. Remember, this is your connection with the Power that runs the whole show and it is limitless. This is its true authentic nature. Attempting to take hold of what *Authentic Personal Power* is would be like attempting to stop yourself in a fast-flowing river. Instead of the water carrying you along, you have now caused a resistance by trying to hold on to something which forces the water to move around you creating a sensation of turbulence.

The experience of this resistance, or this type of effort in your life, is most often felt as suffering. Whenever you misalign yourself with reality, you suffer. This resistance and suffering does not, nor cannot, remove the water from your reality, but it does dramatically shift your experience with the water.

Where does the resistance come from? Resistance arises the moment we live inauthentically. We can do this many, many different ways. Most commonly it is done unconsciously. It occurs just below our awareness that we are doing it. The obvious ways in which you do this are easier to detect and therefore are a little easier to deal with. Some common examples of this could be things like outright lying or working a job which conflicts with your moral sensibilities or going along with friends or family behavior which contradicts your own deeply-held truth. To say these are easier is not meant to imply that they are *easy,* but simply that you are probably more conscious of this type of inauthenticity, which then makes them more accessible.

The deeper roots of inauthenticity stem from much of what I am attempting to clarify here in this book. There is a fundamental misalignment in your perspective of yourself and the world, with what reality actually is. Due to the fact that you see the world and your place in it with such a limited perspective, you behave in ways which are not true to who you really are and what is really going on. Every time you do this, you shift your orientation a little further from truth and create a little more distance from reality and ironically from yourself. To quote a dear friend of mine, David Peters, "Reality has an opinion, too."

You are all familiar with your own opinions, but do you ever take a moment to consider that reality has one, too? And make no mistake about it, reality will have the final say. So, it behooves you to check in with it as often as you can and make course corrections accordingly. To be clear, this "opinion" is not a value judgement, meaning reality doesn't have a preference on what your perspective is, but that reality inevitably is what your perspective is based on. This remains true regardless of how far from reality your current perspective has actually traveled. One of the fundamental truths about reality is that the river of the material world is always moving. All attempts to resist this fact results in an inauthentic experience of what is actually occurring. This will inevitably cause suffering and a distancing in your awareness of your *Authentic Personal Power*.

No matter what your struggles or joys might be in life, to discover your *Authentic Personal Power* is to unlock dimensions within which assure a deeper, richer and more substantial understanding of both.

The Two-Sided Truth

To be authentic is to align yourself with the truth. In order for you to do this, it is essential that you recognize there are two sides to truth. The first is ultimate truth. You can think of this as a macro view. This view remains changeless regardless of circumstance or time. Let's use a tree as a simple example. All trees have roots, a trunk, branches and leaves and all forests are a large area covered with trees. This is ultimately true about all forests and trees, but it leaves out a great deal of detail. You could go further and say it is also ultimately true that all trees need sunlight and water, but as any arborist knows, this also neglects important information such as how much sunlight and water they require to thrive.

The second side is relative truth, which is never completely apart from ultimate truth but can have a significantly different appearance. This side of truth often changes and has a lot to do with where and when we find it. So, with our example of trees and a forest, you might begin your journey toward relative truth by saying something like *this is a deciduous forest.* This would tell you it is primarily filled with trees that seasonally lose their leaves. This is one step away from ultimate truth, because this is not always true about all forests, yet it narrows you down closer to an individual tree. Now let's look at an individual oak tree. At this level, you can get more intimate with all sorts of details which are only true for this individual tree, such as its exact size, shape, health and so on.

This is the micro view. It is important and interesting to note that once you enter the realm of the tree's individual facts, they are all relative to the ultimate truth. The ultimate truth always remains true no matter how detailed you get about a single tree, so though you say that this is a medium-sized oak tree in poor health, it doesn't change the fact that it is located in a deciduous forest, that it must have water and sunlight and that all trees have roots, a trunk, branches and leaves.

In fact, knowing all trees have roots, a trunk, branches and leaves may have been one of the factors that helped you determine the tree was in poor health. Why? Because this particular tree had almost no leaves during the season when it should have been full of leaves. This is a simple way that ultimate truth can help you in a relative way. If you only had relative truth, which is to say, if you only knew how this single tree was, you would not know having a few leaves in the summer was a potential problem.

Authentic

So how does this apply to being authentic? It is imperative that you consider both views on your journey toward uncovering your *Authentic Personal Power,* because keeping both on your radar helps you to check your progress and keep your development balanced and authentic. By this I mean, if you focus too much on relative truth, you might do something like become very focused on your physical body, thinking this is the key to human happiness and fulfilment. On the other hand, if you focus all your attention on the macro view, you may begin to believe the human body is not important at all, because a healthy body is not required for happiness or fulfilment. And this is true. There are many famous, and not famous, examples of people in poor health, with intense physical disabilities, who are far happier and more fulfilled than most who have perfect health.

This ultimate truth does not, however, make the consideration of your body useless or unnecessary. By keeping both present in your attention, you are far more likely to remain balanced, and a balanced system is far more likely to grow healthier and faster.

Why? Because you are remaining truly authentic in a way which aligns with reality. In fact, if it isn't clear already, these two experiences, authenticity and reality, are inseparable. You cannot have one without the other. By focusing all your energy on the physical body, you neglect the reality that you are more than your body. And the same is true if you forget you (at least at this moment) inhabit a body. To be truly authentic, you must attempt to remember both sides of truth so you can remain (to the best of your ability) aligned with reality.

It is most vital to note that another aspect regarding the truth of reality and being authentic with yourself to "the best of your ability" is an important part of the whole understanding of what is going on. In other words, you must also "do your best" to be honest about where you currently are. A simple way to state this is, you can't run before you walk, and though it may be painful to admit, you may still be rolling around on your belly or standing clinging to the couch, not yet ready to let go and take your first step.

There should be NO shame in this. This is where you are, and recognizing it is the key that allows for letting go of the couch (of who you thought you were) so you can find your balance and prepare for your first REAL step toward who you really are! This alignment with reality/truth/authenticity is the most important component to understanding what the *Authentic* part of *Authentic Personal Power* actually means.

Personal

The word personal may seem in conflict with the entire notion of this book, especially the expansion of Perspective 2 (we are not separate), unless you have some understanding of a simple fact—one does not exclude the other. What I am trying to point out here returns to a sentiment put forth in the preface, "… though you are not the world, you are not separate from the world!" This reality is not an either/or fact. Instead, both are true, and because of that, there is more here than either/or thinking could ever understand.

To deeply realize you are a unique manifestation of something far greater than your personal experience could ever contain is to begin to understand the Power that lives within your individual contribution to the world. The Power that dwells within you, that beats your heart and breathes your lungs, is the same Power that inspires a flower to bloom and a tree to delve deep into the earth while at the same time stretching up toward the heavens. Contrary to your common perspective, these things are not separate events, and yet paradoxically, you know you are not the flower and you are not the tree. To hold this paradox quietly, tenderly and intimately within the very fibers of your being is to get in touch with reality as it is, and this gives you access to just how personal this Power is. It is an intimate affair of the highest order and one in which you are endlessly engaged.

Perhaps a more down to earth way to think about this is to consider the outlet receptacle in your home. Each receptacle is unique and occupies an exclusive space in the house. Some outlets have only a single plug, some have several, some are used solely for a specific function, while others serve a more general purpose, but all are connected and derive their power from a single source. This source goes deeper than the panel in your home, deeper than the pole outside your house, deeper than the electric plant which supplies your town. If you are relentless in your pursuit of its origin you will most certainly find that it goes all the way back to the dawn of time. Each of these outlets *are* unique and have certain capabilities, and yes, even certain limits. At the same time each one is inextricably linked, without exception and beyond doubt, to the very fabric of life itself!

This, my dear friend, is true for you, too. The same Power that gave birth to the cosmos gave birth to your *Personal* materialization. Make no mistake, I am not selling a religious point of view or any dogma here—I am only pointing to a simple, honest, hard fact. It is a *Personal* thing to be part of such a significant lineage if you take the time to consider it. It may even begin to dawn on you just how magnificent your inheritance is. Once you accept this inheritance, you may begin to question what you are plugging into the receptacle of your life? The Power waits patiently as potential until you plug into it. Whatever you put your attention and time into is what you are plugging into your life and this will determine what you get from this limitless potential I call the *Authentic Personal Power*.

Power

What is this Power? Of course, this would be a very legitimate question and one I would not blame you for asking. But alas, my honest answer must be…I don't know. To further my honesty, I would have to tell you I don't care. To be clear, I am not implying I don't care about this Power, but rather that I don't care to pin it down. I don't feel the need to limit it in any way. Because once you have actually "tasted the apple," you won't feel the need to overanalyze its origin or exact make up.

Why? Because instead, you prefer to eat the apple and, in the tasting, smelling, chewing and swallowing, all questions are answered. Not because you now know all the answers, but because they no longer seem as relevant as before. You are full. Full of its fragrance, full of its taste, full of the actual touch, sound and sight of it, and this fullness is complete. The mind can rest in this wholeness. This does not mean you cannot inquire into the depths of an apple, but that if you do, you are not attempting to fill some void by doing so. Quite often, you care so much about detail because you are trying to substitute detail for actual experience, and this will always be a severely inadequate replacement.

(Of course, understanding this point is a matter of authenticity, as well, which is to say, this experience cannot be faked, or at least not for long. If you think you are farther along than you actually are, life will show you quickly enough. But you must cultivate a sincere willingness to look. This is an extremely important part of your development. In any form of navigation, you must know where you are to move forward correctly and find your way to the goal. If you are too busy thinking you are already there, you may find yourself stuck in the same place. Conversely, if you are so preoccupied with getting somewhere, you may miss the reality of what the goal is in the first place.)

Another remarkable aspect to Power is you needn't do anything for it to exist. Whether you realize it or not, it is always present. Again, what do you do to breathe your lungs, pump your heart or create oxygen? Nothing. Thankfully, you don't need to do anything for all this to happen. It does so on its own accord. It is supplied for you. The list of events, elements and matter which had to occur so you could read this book would be so long it could fill fifty more books of this size and still not scratch the surface of its magnitude.

Please take a minute to contemplate what you just read. There is no absence in reality—only abundance. Only Presence. To let this in is to let go of fear. You are not alone. You are not separate. You are cared for in the most elaborate way possible. You are inextricably linked to this entire affair. The whole universe was organized to create you. This is not meant to imply that life is always *good*, or even *fair*, but instead that life is pregnant with opportunity.

The most significant opportunity being the one I am trying to point to right now. It is the one shared by all, regardless of our financial, social and even physical condition. It is the opportunity to recognize this very Power within you. It is not a matter of doing anything, because you already possess it. You simply need to recognize, or *reclaim*, your awareness of something that is always present.

Try it right now. Look outside a window at a tree, or at a pet lying near you or, better yet, look at your own hand. Look at it. I mean really gaze into it as if you have never seen it before. Don't think about it. Feel it with your entire body. Can you feel the majesty, the mystery, the wonder of it all?

If you struggle with this, try noticing the space around whatever you are looking at. Notice how the emptiness is an integral part of your hand or the tree or the animal and how it participates in its physical presence. The space around it holds it perfectly and allows it to be exactly as it is— no judgement, no hinderance, no requirements, simply space to let it be what it is.

Why? Because it is perfect. What do I mean by perfect? Exactly that. It is perfect, the space, the tree, the animal and your hand. Perfect! In need of nothing more. Now I understand very well this is a giant leap for many of us, but it is nonetheless true. How can I say this with such certainty? Because it is so. The tree, the animal and your hand exist, and in their existence, they are precisely as they are meant to be. To argue with this simple fact would be to believe you know how to run this whole show. It is glaringly obvious to me that we wouldn't have the foggiest idea how to hold the universe together. Let's remember we don't even know how to operate vital organs in our own body let alone run the entire universe. This doesn't make us powerless, in fact, it gets us in contact with our *Authentic Personal Power* because we have connected with what part is ours and what is shared.

If you don't like something about reality, you are free to try to change it, but first it is best if you take a good hard look at reality for what it is as clearly and wholly as possible. Then, you can determine what—if anything—should be done. It may also be helpful to realize change is a curious thing, because it is always occurring. Each of these things—the tree, the animal, your hand—have already changed since the reading of these last few sentences and, oddly enough, they have again found themselves in a state of perfection.

To understand this deeply is to remove the air that fear uses to breathe. When you cannot accept what is before you as it is, you separate yourself from the Power of reality. This invites fear to enter and fill the void. What then follows is the use of force as a replacement for Power, and this is an unfortunate substitute indeed.

Again, this does not mean you cannot or should not work toward changing things you see as needing change. It is to point out that where you come from when you seek change determines what success and longevity you may hope to achieve. If you are coming from a place of absence (which is a result of fear or a void), you can be sure you will be applying force. Force is what most of our human history has been forged upon, and it's why so little of it has lasted. If you come from a place of Presence (which is the perfection or abundance of reality) you align yourself with Power, and this is the same Power that created the whole shebang. (More on this in Perspective 4). You may summarize this as "the means are the ends." Fear is the root cause of force, and it comes from a sense of absence or not enough. When we come from this place, we can be sure there will never be enough. To be sure this "never enough" feeling is the energy which motivates most of us and is responsible for addiction, anxiety, depression, anger and a long list of other limiting human tendencies, but this is not our home. This is not where you find your true Self, if only you took the time to look.

You are intimately and indivisibly connected to the entirety of this world, which operates on the principle of perfection. To be clear, I am not talking about perfection in regard to your own personal desires or concerns, but on the level of it being precisely as it needs to be. To perceive this perfection is to let go of how you might think something *should* be, it is also to loosen your grip on the way you *want* something to be. You do this so you might clearly see how the thing actually is and to pay homage to it. It took an entire cosmos to create it, whatever "it" is, and this should not be taken lightly, but reverently. Once you have cultivated this type of context, you can then consider what might be done about changing it.

Insight and Consent

So much of what you consider to be change is nothing more than gaining a certain level of clarity and then allowing that insight (i.e., inner sight or accurate and deep intuitive understanding) to stimulate a natural response. Again, if you see a bus coming at you, you move out of the way. If you see clearly and fully what you are doing and why, your behavior instinctively shifts.

One of the surest ways to obstruct this organic process is to attempt to force it. On the other hand, consent is the *best* way to get in touch with your *Authentic Personal Power* because it has a completely different orientation than force. The origin of the word *consent,* which is *con* "together" and *sentire* "feel" literally means to feel together or connected.

To what? To your Power! When you put these two ingredients together—insight and consent—you can be assured you are aligning yourself with the Power of the natural world, which is change. This change may come swiftly, or it may arrive unhurried, but you can know in your consenting heart that it is indeed happening, and that you are irrefutably and inseparably a part of it all!

Contemplation for Expanding Perspective 3

If I am what I fear
than I am nothing
for there is nothing in fear
but fear itself.

Surely, fear comes from an absence
a deficiency in what is.
But how can this be?

How can what is
be less than it is?
What is
is everything.

All that is
is complete.

All that is
is what I am

for I can be no more or less

than that
and to find the line
where I stop
and everything else starts
is like chasing the horizon —

its end will never be found.

For the Power
that moves the stars through the heavens,
pumps the paradise of my heart,
pulls the trees towards their dreams,
and washes the shorelines
with countless stirrings from the ocean.

How in the midst of all this
should I fear?

Only when I forget that I am That
Only when I entertain absence
Only when I enter the confusion

of mistaking who I am
as someone alone
alone in the cage of my six senses.

To be sure
I shall stumble
and fall prey to fear
and forget
again, and again
but just as certain –

No more so!

I shall find the truth

Seeing Beyond

of who I am waiting for me
patiently, endlessly, tenderly
reminding me
to *See Beyond* what I can see

into the depths
and glory
of what has always been
present
in plain view
as me
as You.

Exercises for Expanding Perspective 3

-1-

Think of a loved one who has passed away, be they a parent, grandparent, friend, a pet, or a coworker of whom you were fond of. See if it isn't true that a small piece of them lives on within you. Not just the memory of them, but some ineffable quality which in a strange way encapsulates who they were in the time they graced your life. Is it not true that this is a part of them which can never die? See if you can't discover how they reside everywhere now that they have left their body. They occupy a place in your heart, exactly as they did when they were alive. You are not physically with them, but now this space is even greater! Why? Because now they live in the rustling of the trees, or the color of the sunset, or the movement of the water or in one of their favorite spots, items or past times. Don't take this as poetic musing. See if you can't find them there. Sincerely search for them in things which moved their heart and now move yours and see if you can't feel their reality. They are as real as they ever were. If you wish you could speak to them, then by all means do so. Find a private place and have a conversation with them. Listen deep within and you will hear their reply. How? Because they live within you. Nothing and no one are ever truly gone—they only change form. Yes, this may be a challenge for you to understand, but if you sincerely search, you will find this to be true. In this discovery, you find that all of life is in perfect continuity, and in this a great gift is given, one which comes at a high cost but that changes the landscape of your soul because now you know without doubt there is nothing to fear from death. "Life has no opposite. The opposite of death is birth. Life is eternal." Eckhart Tolle

-2-

Purchase a journal (if you don't already have one) and set aside some time this week to spend with yourself. Before we talk about what you might write, first let me propose how you might sit down with yourself to do this work. Think of yourself as a lover or dear close friend or a sibling, someone for whom you would do anything. Someone for whom you would sacrifice time, money and hardship and be here for yourself in that same way. Be patient and tender with yourself as you explore how you feel and what you need. Now write down one of your biggest fears. Simply write it down and look at it. Don't judge yourself or get carried away with the emotion of it. Simply look at what you have written. Now allow yourself to talk about why you have this fear and where you think it may have come from. Write down everything you want to say about it even if it feels as if you are rambling, and even if you aren't sure whether it is relevant. Be honest with yourself, and at the same time, gentle. There is no right or wrong thing you can write here. You are merely investigating how you feel and think. No one else need ever read this, so let it all out. Once you have exhausted everything you need to say, write five things for which you are grateful, whether they are about this particular subject or not. Now say these five things out loud and then close your journal. Let it all go and see how you feel. Simply be quiet with it for a few moments and then go on with your day. Revisit this writing in about a week or so and see if you feel different about anything you find there. If so, then write down what is different and why. If not, then sit with yourself like a friend. Have compassion (not pity) for yourself and listen to your heart as it longs to tell you something.

-3-

Meditate for 15-20 minutes every day for a week. Find a comfortable and quiet place and sit with your back straight and hands resting effortlessly in your lap. Close your eyes and take three conscious deep breaths, allowing each breath to settle you further into your body and deeper into relaxation. As your breathing finds its own natural rhythm, cultivate a sense of complete resolution, which is to say that you are fully resolved to be here right now, however you find yourself. You are not attempting to accomplish anything, nor are you trying to be perfectly still. You are simply sitting with an acute sense of curiosity. Ask yourself, *Who am I? Who asks such a question?* You are not trying to answer this question as much as get a sense of who it is who might ask such a thing. *What in me has the means to ponder such a peculiar thought? Am I more than this thought? Am I more than any emotion I might be experiencing?* Look without judging and without the need for an answer. Simply look as if you were gazing into still water and trying to discover its contents. You are not invested in what you might find in these deep waters, only innocently curious. The mystery of you lurks there and will become visible when you allow what has clouded the waters to settle. Clarity is so simple that it requires no movement to perceive it, only a sincere openness and willingness to see who you really are…and it is Perfect. Spend some time here without worry or concern about whether you are doing it right. Just be with yourself, quietly and tenderly. That is enough.

Epilogue

These three perspectives are fundamental and carry within them the ability to build a strong foundation for your life once you understand their potential and nuance. "It only takes a single matchstick to start a forest fire" says the Indian sage Papaji, and this is so true. Though there are four more perspectives to explore, you should not rush the digestion of these first three. If you truly understand even one of them, the rest will begin to fall into place and your life will be set on fire. A fire that will light the way. These books have been kept small by design in hopes that you might read them more than once with the belief that *repetition is not redundancy* and that as you contemplate these matters, depth is gained which would be otherwise unavailable. Repetition is how you learn, and even though the heart of which I am pointing is not learnable, it is discoverable. By returning to these fundamental perspectives again and again, you may unearth things you somehow managed to overlook before.

It is true you can achieve the same result with a single act of complete surrender. If you are willing to let go of all you thought you were, stand naked and humble as the prodigal son upon his return, you will experience the reality of union—but this approach is uncommon and rare.

Personally, I have found my way very slowly. Sometimes I have questioned whether anything was happening at all, only to discover (with hindsight) that each moment was a precious unfolding which for some unforeseeable reason was necessary. Perhaps this is why I recommend a slow approach, because it has been my experience. But I have also watched many others time and time again make what appear to be incredible lunges forward only to fall back then lunge again, only to stumble again, and with the final result of giving up. This seems a pity, when these people obviously have interest and aptitude but were merely missing a key ingredient. This key ingredient is probably best summarized in the child's tale of the tortoise and the hare. I am here to testify that slow and steady, my friend, is real.

The Law of Dissidence (Perspective 4) which is explored with great detail in the sequel to this book might be simply stated as follows- *if we push too hard, we get a push back.* It serves us well to be mindful of this law. When untying a tangled cord; it is best we do so gently. Otherwise, we tend to tighten the knot and make our work even harder. To *See Beyond* what can be seen is a gift that is given freely if "we have eyes to see," and this requires only one thing from us—a sincere willingness to look. I wish for you the grace of seeing the truth, because with this sight, we do not cling to an answer, but rather find glory in the question. This creates an unexpected blend of humility and confidence which fashions within us a contagious Joy and eternal hope.

"Be patient toward all that is unsolved in your heart and try to love the questions themselves, like locked rooms and like books that are now written in a very foreign tongue. Do not now seek the answers, which cannot be given you because you would not be able to live them. And the point is, to live everything. Live the questions now. Perhaps you will then gradually, without noticing it, live along some distant day into the answer." - Rainer Maria Rilke

ACKNOWLEDGMENTS

This book is the result of countless occurrences and connections which are beyond my conscious reckoning but there certainly are many that I am aware of - I owe so much of what I am to my mother, Anna's Love and my father, Danny's discipline the blend of which proved to be just what was needed. My two sisters, Leah and Shanna, you have always been an inspiration and motivation to me, not least of which because of how you have always looked at me. My children Sage, Elijah and Jade without whose innocence, patience and beauty I would not know the meaning of commitment. To Jerry Ryan, the teacher who introduced me to Hermann Hesse and nurtured my deep early longings through excellent literature. To *Sounds True Publishing* for all the transformational content you produce. I hope to be among the list one day! To Manny Hernandez for our talk on the beach and your constant encouragement. To Chris Armfield for the endurance, insight and creativity that produced such a stunning and inspiring book cover. To Nathan Hassall for editing my poetry which quickly provoked deep furtive inner attachments. And to my wife, Shell who is a never-ending source of awe, inspiration and guidance proving that there truly are angels and you can wake beside one every morning, never tiring from the sight of their sleeping eyes, disheveled hair and naked feet. You are my muse!

ABOUT THE AUTHOR

After reading a Hermann Hesse book at the age of fourteen, Adrien Fiorucci experienced his first pull to a higher calling through what proved to be the seeds of an awakening. Never forgetting this early revelation, he spent most of the next thirty-plus years as a small business owner and general contractor. Throughout his daily struggles with addiction, depression and anger which served as a motivating backdrop to his spiritual pursuits, Fiorucci discovered that the mystical dwelled within everyday practical living. Following no direct teacher or religion, Fiorucci slowly and consistently surrendered to the draw of the "still, small voice". After making various positive changes to his life, he experienced several deeper awakenings which compelled him to step into the public arena as a spiritual teacher and write a series of books. Fiorucci demonstrates that, if he can experience such a profound shift to *What's Real* in the midst of an ordinary yet challenging life, so can you!

To book Adrien for speaking engagements and to learn more about his work Visit: www.whatsrealwaf.com

Made in the USA
Middletown, DE
26 December 2019